BOO

Writt
and Ma
Translated by Jessica Foster
and Rebecca Neal

The Road

BY CORMAC MCCARTHY

Bright
≡Summaries.com

CORMAC MCCARTHY

AMERICAN WRITER

- **Born in Providence (Rhode Island) in 1933.**
- **Notable works:**
  - *The Orchard Keeper* (1965), novel
  - *All the Pretty Horses* (1992), novel
  - *No Country for Old Men* (2005), novel

The American author Cormac McCarthy was born in Providence, Rhode Island, in 1933, and is considered to be one of the most significant authors of his generation. His novels are mostly about the inherent violence of American society and are characterised by a pronounced sense of pessimism. He has written a number of novels, including *All the Pretty Horses* (1992), which received both the National Book Award and the National Book Critics Circle Award that year.

No Country for Old Men (2005), which is about drug trafficking in Texas, was successfully adapted for film by the Coen brothers (Joel, born in 1954, and Ethan, born in 1957) in 2007. The film won four Oscars, including the award for Best Picture.

THE ROAD

THE ADVENTURES OF A FATHER AND SON IN A POSTAPOCALYPTIC WORLD

- **Genre:** novel
- **Reference edition:** McCarthy, C. (2010) *The Road*. London: Picador.
- **1st edition:** 2006
- **Themes:** violence, humanity, family, death, survival, apocalypse

The Road, which was first published in the USA in 2006, is Cormac McCarthy's most recent novel. It tells the story of a father and son's travels through a postapocalyptic wasteland, and has two features in particular which set it apart from the rest of the author's work. Firstly, the violence featured in *The Road* is much more extreme, and it transcends the boundaries of American society to give the novel a metaphysical and universal dimension. Secondly, story's surprisingly optimistic ending seems to suggest that redemption is possible for humankind.

The novel was extremely well received by critics and readers alike. It won the Pulitzer Prize in 2007 and was adapted for the cinema by John Hillcoat (Australian film director, born in 1961) in 2009.

SUMMARY

A WORLD IN RUINS

In a world where society has collapsed in the wake of a disaster, the nature of which is left vague, a nameless father and son set off for the southern United States in order to escape the harsh winter. The father draws on all his skill and courage to make the best of the situation for the sake of his son, who was born after the natural disaster. The child's mother committed suicide after giving birth to him. To begin with, the father told his son stories about the way the world was before the catastrophe and tried to extol the values of solidarity and humanism, but now he has nothing left to talk about.

Furthermore, hordes of cannibals roam the country, and the father and son come across some on their way. They must therefore be constantly on their guard and remain hidden. They do not know the date or their precise location, and navigate using the position of the sun in the sky.

They are alone, carrying various objects with them in a rucksack and a supermarket trolley: jars, some tools, blankets, tarpaulins, children's toys and a revolver loaded with two bullets. Most of their possessions have been scavenged from the roadside. They are both dirty, gaunt and terrified.

In order to survive, they will have to cross the mountains within four days, despite the bitter cold. They have almost nothing left to eat: the father wants to give his food to his child, but the boy refuses. One day, they come across a man in rags lying prone on the ground. The child wants to help him by staying with him and giving him food, but the father says no.

While they are sleeping in a forest, they are awoken by the sound of a group of men passing by in a truck. They hide, knowing that they could be cannibals, but one of the men finds them by chance and grabs the child. The father kills the man and they manage to escape. Later on, the father goes to find the trolley that they abandoned when they ran away, but all their possessions have been stolen. The loss of their blankets and provisions leaves the father and son more impoverished than ever.

THE CANNIBALS

Two days later, they reach a town where they see signs of human life. Despite the risks, they go into the town to look for something to eat, but find nothing. They decide to spend the night in a car, where they will be hidden while they sleep, and resume their search in the morning. The following day, the child thinks he has seen a little boy and a dog in the distance. He clings to this hope and wants to find them, but the father decides to move on.

They have no more water and can no longer make a fire as they do not want to attract attention. One day, while they are hiding at the side of the road, they see a group of men go past, followed by women and children with their hands tied. It is a horde of cannibals and their future victims.

They continue walking, and it begins to snow. When they find shelter in a burnt-out forest, the trees begin to fall down around them, forcing them to keep moving. The father puts together makeshift shoes from plastic bags and pieces of anorak. Having barely eaten or slept for five days, they arrive in a small town and break into a house, where they find abundant provisions and blankets. However, they also discover imprisoned men, women and children under a trapdoor in the house, who beg for their help. When a group of cannibals arrives, the father and son flee and hide in the undergrowth.

THE ILLNESS

The child falls ill: "He looked like something out of a death camp" (p. 123). The father finds drinking water and some old apples on a farm, then they set off again. They experience their toughest night yet, unable to light a fire and drenched by the rain.

A few days later, as the spectre of death looms ever larger, the father discovers an isolated house near a village; after inspecting it, he notices a trapdoor in the garden, which leads to a nuclear bomb shelter. Inside, they find enough supplies and tools to ensure their survival. They spend a few peaceful days in this makeshift home, taking the time to build their strength back up.

When they leave again with their supplies replenished, the father estimates that they are about 200 miles from the coast. They come across a tramp. At the child's insistence, they give him some food, then spend the night with him by the fire. The father asks the old man questions, but he never answers. He says "There's no God and we are his prophets" (p. 182). They leave the man to his fate.

They continue their journey, like "two hunted animals" (p. 138), "street addicts" (p. 188) or "fugitives" (p. 198). The father, who was already coughing, falls ill and is now spitting blood, which forces them to stay in the same place for four days. This disease will turn out to be fatal.

In the distance they see an encampment of three men and a pregnant woman, but by the time they arrive, they have all left. There is a child on a spit over the fire. They then arrive in a village and set up camp in a luxurious house, where they find things to eat and to wash with. They stay there for four days.

THE OCEAN

By the time they reach the ocean, they have next to no supplies left. The sea is not blue, but black, and the landscape looks like all the others they have passed through: grey, cold and lifeless. Further down the embankment, the father finds countless fish skeletons.

They discover a ship 300 metres from the beach. The father swims out to it several times to look for supplies, leaving the child alone. He finds food and a flare gun. That evening, he fires the gun, trying to set off a flare, but the light only weakly pierces the ash cloud that the sky has become. Then the child falls ill too, and they are forced to stay on the beach for three days.

When they briefly leave their camp, they come back to find that it has been ransacked. Fortunately, they find the thief, whom the father threatens with his weapon, and recover their belongings. They then set off again. They arrive at a port and are targeted by a man armed with a bow and arrow. The father is seriously wounded in the leg, but manages to shoot the man with the flare gun.

They then take refuge in a block of flats, where the father tries to stitch up his wound before they press on again. Winter has arrived, and the father, who has not recovered from his illness, is on his last legs. It is therefore left to the child to set up camp and find food. When the father dies, the child stays by his side for three days. When he sets off again, he meets a man who offers to accompany him. The child hesitates before accepting. The man has two children and a wife who comforts the orphan.

CHARACTER STUDY

THE FATHER

We do not know his name or much about his physical appearance. All we know is that he has a beard and dishevelled hair, plus the information we glean through his memories: he mentions the place where he grew up, in a small town not far from a fishing lake, and reflects on the death of his wife after she gave birth and his own refusal to die.

He has nobody in the world but his son, and is defined by his relationship with him. He appears to be an extremely attentive, gentle, protective, decisive father who is willing to sacrifice himself for his child's sake. He also possesses the necessary skills to ensure their survival. For example, he has a knack for finding food and tools: "In an old batboard smokehouse they found a ham gambreled up in a high corner" (p. 16); "He kicked a cleared place in the snow out where the fire wouldn't set the tree alight and he carried wood from the other trees, breaking of the limbs and shaking away the snow" (p. 100).

His love for his son is the only thing that gives his life meaning and stops him from wanting to die: "the boy was all that stood between him and death" (p. 29). Indeed, the call of death is constant, as he knows that life is now hopeless. He believes that he is lying to himself by clinging to hope and his desire to live, but he forces himself to do so for his son's sake. He often views his son as a godlike figure, as he sees him as the embodiment of hope and innocence, and the only symbol of a possible future.

He keeps the two bullets in his gun at all times to be sure that he can end his and his son's lives if the situation worsens even further.

THE CHILD

We do not know the name of the child either, as he is simply referred to as "the boy". We also do not know his exact age, but he cannot be any younger than six (he can walk alone for long periods of time, light a fire by himself and use a gun to defend himself). He was born after the cataclysm, so he never knew the world before and even doubts that it ever existed. As with his father, we know next to nothing about his physical appearance: all we know is that they are both thin, dirty and dressed in rags.

The novel gives us less information about the child's thoughts than those of his father: we never get a glimpse of his dreams, and the omniscient narrator generally seems to keep a certain amount of distance from him: "The boy took one last look back at the cart and then followed him" (p. 105); "You know that, don't you? The boy stood looking down. He lowered his head" (p. 52). Most of the time, only the boy's actions are described, and his thoughts remain inscrutable to us.

What we learn about him generally comes from discussions with his father, through which we become aware of his almost constant fear and his obedience to his father. However, we are also shown that his father has instilled a desire to do good in him: when he meets survivors, he insists on helping them every time.

> "Can't we help him? Papa?
> No. We can't help him.

The boy kept pulling at his coat. Papa? he said. Stop it. Can't we help him papa?" (p. 51)

As we see in the episodes with the man who has been knocked down, the thief and the old blind man, the boy is eager to help everyone he comes across.

These two anonymous heroes therefore have no unique traits or identifying characteristics; they are just a father and son like any other. This anonymity gives them a universal dimension, and is also perhaps used to show that human traits like appearance and personality are erased in this inhuman world, in which individuals are reduced to their survival instinct and everything else is secondary.

THE CANNIBALS

Like the story's two protagonists, the cannibals are not described physically; everything that we know about them comes from the father and son's wanderings. They are savages who roam in packs to hunt the isolated survivors, which forces the father and son to stay on the run indefinitely. Once they have been captured, the men, women and children who fall into the cannibals' hands never make it out alive.

They play a fundamental role in the story's plot, as it is because of them that the main characters have to stay in hiding. Whether he is searching for food or looking for shelter that will provide some degree of comfort, the father is constantly alert to the possibility of an attack.

The cannibals are depicted as savage and almost monstrous. Like zombies, which are a staple of postapocalyptic literature, they inspire a primal fear in the characters:

> "Shh, he said. Shh.
> Are they going to kill us? Papa?
> Shh.
> They lay in the leaves and the ash with their hearts pounding." (p. 118)

The cannibals symbolise evil and the worst elements of humanity, and are set in direct opposition to the little boy, who represents the last vestige of hope in the face of terror and degeneration. He still has faith in humanity, in spite of the terror that the cannibals inspire in him. He pays no heed to the danger inherent in any encounter with other people, and always tries to help those he comes across, such as the old beggar, the man who has been knocked down and even the thief.

ANALYSIS

A POSTAPOCALYPTIC NOVEL?

The best-known authors of postapocalyptic or dystopian fiction include the American novelists Richard Matheson (1926-2013) with *I Am Legend* (1954), Stephen King (born in 1947) with *The Stand* (1978) and Max Brooks (born in 1972) with *World War Z: An Oral History of the Zombie War* (2006), and the British writers Mary Shelley (1797-1851) with *The Last Man* (1826) and George Orwell (1903-1950) with *1984* (1949). A number of French authors, such as Robert Merle (1908-2004) with *Malevil* (1972) and Pierre Bordage (born in 1955) with *Les Derniers Hommes* ("The Last Men", 2002), have also written postapocalyptic novels.

Postapocalyptic fiction tends to describe a declining world in which trauma has become an inescapable part of life. In this world, society as we know it has disappeared and been replaced by a much more violent reality, shaped by threats such as deadly viruses which decimate the population, nuclear attacks or natural disasters.

This decline is made even more nightmarish by the attendant surge in hatred and inhumanity, which are depicted as an inherent part of human nature but are brought out into the open by the postapocalyptic situation.

At first glance, it seems clear that *The Road* is a postapocalyptic novel: we are given to understand that the world it describes has been devastated by a nuclear disaster, and the survivors form armed, cannibalistic gangs that rampage across the landscape. This brutal postapocalyptic society has its own unwritten rules, which the father and son must follow if they want to survive.

However, although the novel clearly displays many of the key characteristics of postapocalyptic fiction, it departs from the conventions of the genre in that it does not describe or provide any substantive information about the catastrophe itself, which is alluded to briefly and left in the past. This unusual narrative choice makes the novel atypical of the genre and allows it to transcend the codes of postapocalyptic fiction: depicting the decline of the world without discussing its cause in detail allows McCarthy to focus on the horror of the two protagonists' situation and the violence that stalks them at every moment.

The Road is permeated by violence, notably through the novel's unusual depiction of time and space. Given that the protagonists' main concern is finding the food they need to stay alive, time and distance are measured by the gaps between meals, and time in the narrative is mainly spent waiting. The question of when they will find food is constantly just below the surface of the story. Time in the novel is therefore cyclical, as they repeat the same pattern: looking for food, walking, finding food and starting over again, with no end in sight. This cycle can be seen as violent because of the gnawing hunger that dogs the protagonists and poses a real and constant threat to their lives.

This repetition and the novel's distinctive treatment of space mean that it also has some similarities with the western. In this genre, and in a number of McCarthy's novels, the frontier is a key theme and serves to evoke the idea of a journey and of new horizons to conquer. The frontier plays an essential role in *The Road*: the father and son's primary aim is to reach and cross this geographical boundary to reach the south, where they hope to find land that has escaped the destruction wreaked by the catastrophe and the violence it has engendered.

The object of conquest is therefore the wilderness, a pure, Edenic space that has not been corrupted by humanity. The two protagonists are not only trying to outrun the cannibals and find food; they are also making their way towards the coast, because the sea represents the hope of nature untouched by the catastrophe.

This wilderness stands in stark contrast to the space they are forced to inhabit: "He said that everything depended on reaching the coast, yet waking in the night he knew that all of this was empty and no substance to it. There was a good chance they would die in the mountains and that would be that" (p. 29).

Nature is ultimately a disturbing presence in *The Road*. Even the slowly dying trees become a deadly threat to the father and son:

> "Come on. We have to move.
> What is it?

It's the trees. They're falling down." (p. 102)

In traditional westerns, the American wilderness is conceived as Edenic, but in *The Road* it becomes horrific.

INTERTEXTUALITY

The Road is undeniably an original novel, but it nonetheless draws inspiration from earlier works. Its title recalls the 1957 novel *On the Road* (1957) by Jack Kerouac (American writer and leading figure of the Beat Generation, 1922-1969), and the similarities between the two novels are striking. Specifically, both authors depict characters who are fleeing in an attempt to escape from society and the established order. However, the societies they depict differ significantly: while Kerouac described the America of the 1950s, McCarthy depicts an imaginary world that is based on reality (indeed, postapocalyptic fiction has a number of features in common with science fiction).

Perhaps the real significance of the link between the two novels comes from their differing approach to the same subject. McCarthy subverts the frontier myth and depicts the fundamental sterility of American society, and in his novel there is no hope that the original frontier can be pushed back any further. Conversely, Kerouac saw the possibility for movement and change, and believed that future generations could drive back the frontier.

The Road can also be compared to other works, such as Richard Matheson's novel *I Am Legend*. The two books' subject matter is similar, as they both follow survivors who are threatened by a terrifying "other" (the marauding bands of cannibals in *The Road*, and mutants and zombies in *I Am Legend*), and they both depict survivors who safeguard the social and moral values of the world prior to the disaster. The father in *The Road* refers to this as "carrying the fire" (p. 87), while the main character of *I Am Legend* is the last person who is able to create a vaccination against the deadly disease that has spread around the world.

A PARED-DOWN NARRATIVE

Perhaps the most striking thing about the novel is its sparseness. There are only two protagonists, neither of whom is named, very few unexpected developments and a simple plot: a father and son travelling south. This economy is certainly appropriate to illustrate the extent to which life has been wiped out in this devastated world, where every day is the same, and seems to represent an eternity with no hope of remembering the past or moving forward into the future.

In this setting, language is in a state of crisis: words are lacking because reality is lacking. With the human world destined to disappear, "[t]he sacred idiom [is] shorn of its referents and so of its reality" (p. 93). Consequently, the style is simple, pared-down, rudimentary and devoid of any embellishment, much like the world it describes. Verbs are omitted from many phrases, perhaps as a way of signifying the impossibility of action.

Additionally, the omniscient narrator does not provide any commentary or analysis; instead, they merely report the facts using free indirect speech, combining their words with those of the characters: "They stood in the road and studied it. I think we should check it out, the man said. Take a look. The weeds they forded fell to dust about them" (p. 4).

The father and the child speak to each other, but only for practical purposes. Over the course of the novel the child, who never knew the world before the apocalypse, becomes increasingly reluctant to communicate, withdrawing further into silence with each new challenge they face. This is a worrying prospect, as the loss of language means the loss of humanity, history and faith: "On this road there are no godspoke men" (p. 32). However, we are also told that, in this world, even "the silence was breathless" (p. 103).

There are several phrases that are repeated almost like a refrain throughout the novel, and which signify above all the connection and the bond between the father and son. They are phrases that the son has picked up from his father, which he repeats without really understanding their meaning: "We have to keep looking" (p. 84), "And we're carrying the fire" (p. 136) or even "Okay", that strange notion of agreement, which seems as though it could apply to both the father's words and the world itself.

A COMING-OF-AGE STORY: PASSING ON THE BATON

The novel only features two characters and particularly emphasises the strength of the relationship between father and son: they are "each the other's world entire" (p. 4). Each of them is wholly dependent on the other: the child because he could not protect himself and survive alone, and the father because the child is his only reason to keep living. They only exist because of each other, and for each other. They are also each other's "world entire" because the child forces the father to imagine a different future and a different world, and because the father strives to tell the child stories of a better world, like the one before the catastrophe.

Through his stories, fictional tales and real memories, the father describes a world full of life and games to his son, a world in which good people received the rewards they deserved and were happy. Above all, he strives to impart the values of good and evil to him. His stories therefore allow him to pass on human values, and humanity itself, in a world devoid of these qualities. The father also teaches his child the tricks and techniques needed to survive.

He sometime talks about his memories from the world before the catastrophe. For example, when he finds his childhood home, he says: "On cold winter nights when the electricity was out in a storm we would sit at the fire here, me and my sisters, doing our homework" (p. 26). The boy also asks his father to tell him stories: "You can read me a story, the boy said. Can't you, Papa?" (p. 6). These stories are always happy ones, and are used to convey hope.

The father also teaches the boy essential survival techniques for the new world. Each of his actions and all of the objects or tools he uses are very precisely described in the novel:

> "He pulled the bolt and bored out the collet with a hand drill and resleeved it with a section of pipe he'd cut to length with a hacksaw. Then he bolted it all back together and stood the cart upright and wheeled it around the floor. It ran fairly true. The boy sat watching everything." (pp. 15-16)

Finally, through this novel about passing things

on, the author seems to invite us to reflect on the role and meaning of stories in general, and maybe of this novel in particular. Through the *mise en abyme* technique, the characters discuss what it means to tell a story. In this way, we are shown that the role of the novel and of stories is to preserve and propagate humanity in an inhuman world.

> "[Child:] You always tell happy stories.
> [Father:] You don't have any happy ones?
> They're more like real life.
> But my stories are not.
> Your stories are not. No.
> [...] Well, I think we're still here. A lot of bad things have happened but we're still here."
> (p. 288)

The meaning of most stories is made clear by their ending, which can be happy or unhappy. Since *The Road* ends on a hopeful note, which could be interpreted as a happy ending, it goes some way toward refuting the boy's belief that all stories have unhappy endings. In other words, the father was not wrong to use his stories to remind his son that there is good to be found in the world.

THE METAPHYSICAL DIMENSION OF THE NOVEL

The postapocalyptic world the characters live in has stripped them of everything apart from the most primal aspect of their being: the survival instinct that each individual possesses, which works to prevent the extinction of the species. Everything that made the world human has disappeared, leaving only the terrifying truth that humans are fragile and insignificant beings.

Thus, in the novel, history and geography are no more, and the seasons that set the rhythm of human life have disappeared, as have the moon and the sun. Moreover, the novel is utterly devoid of any other signs of life: there are no animals, no birds, no sound, not even wind; the world is frozen in an endless moment in time, in which death is the only possible future and hope has already died. The only thing that remains in this ruined world is survival instinct, which is absurd and senseless, because human lives are ultimately meaningless.

The Road also evokes the myth of Sisyphus. In the

Odyssey, Homer (Greek poet, 8th century BCE) described the punishment of Sisyphus, who was punished for having deceived the gods by being condemned to roll a boulder up a hill just to see it fall down again for all eternity. The story of Sisyphus has been interpreted by Albert Camus (French writer, 1913-1960) in his essay *The Myth of Sisyphus* (1942) as an allegory of the absurdity of human existence, given that we are always destined to repeat the same actions in vain.

Indeed, as the title indicates, the plot of McCarthy's novel consists of a single repeated action, that of setting off. The main characters set off every day, all the while knowing that they only thing their journey will ever lead them to is death. Consequently, their epic journey seems absurd. Although the father wants to make his son believe that better days are coming, in reality he has little hope, which means that there is nothing to really justify the journey they are embarking on. It is a journey that was supposed to lead to the south, but in reality the only thing it leads to is the father's death.

The Road can also be interpreted as the search for a lost paradise, namely the world as it was before the catastrophe. This was a human, colourful, lively, noisy world, which the father remembers fondly and describes. The two protagonists are sustained and guided by their faint hope of rediscovering this past.

The novel also helps us to understand childhood as another lost paradise. This is firstly because the father puts his son on a pedestal, giving every one of the boy's words and gestures the power of a sacred commandment; and secondly because he recognises several times that, without the child, he would certainly have already committed suicide. Childhood thus becomes a symbol of life, as the child shields his father from death and despair. Adulthood, on the other hand, is the age of giving up (the boy's mother committed suicide), lies and mistrust (the old man), and inhumanity (the cannibals).

THE METAPHOR OF RELIGION

In addition to these metaphysical elements, the novel also has a religious dimension. The search for a lost paradise is more than a search for the world as it was before the disaster; it is also a way of gaining redemption through faith.

A religious metaphor, in which the child is depicted as a messenger from God, runs throughout the novel. The father clings to his son and sees him as a sort of messiah. For example, he describes his hair by saying "Golden chalice, good to house a god" (p. 78), and seems to think that his role is to protect this representative of God: "My job is to take care of you. I was appointed to do that by God" (p. 80).

Furthermore, the two characters' journey seems to represent a   true vocation for them: the father tells his son that they are "carrying the fire" (p. 87), and this fire could symbolise faith on earth, which is preserved and carried by the child so that it can be passed on.

> "Maybe he believes in God.
> I don't know what he believes in.
> He'll get over it.
> No he won't." (p. 185)

In this excerpt, the father is talking to the old beggar whom the boy wanted to invite to eat with them. While the beggar seems to have lost his faith in God, his son's optimism means that the father cannot stop believing. This creates an implicit parallel between the hope embodied by the boy and religious faith. The child believes in humankind's inherent goodness without asking for anything in return, in the same way that believers believe in God and put all their faith in Him.

When considered in light of this religious metaphor, the father and son's long walk takes on a prophetic dimension: "All of this like some ancient anointing. So be it. Evoke the forms. When you've nothing else construct ceremonies out of the air and breathe upon them" (pp. 77-78). The child seems to represent more than just hope; he can be viewed as the last vestige of faith in a devastated world. Specifically, he represents faith in human beings, faith in the essential goodness of humankind, and faith in a god who will guide them to a better world in the south.

The ending of *The Road* contrasts with the bleak events of the narrative, as it implies that God is present in some form through the child: "She [the boy's adoptive mother] would talk to him sometimes about God. He tried to talk to God but the best thing was to talk to his father and he did talk to him and he didn't forget" (p. 306).

The Road can be summarised as a postapocalyptic novel written in a pared-down style which depicts a father and son's quest for survival. However, McCarthy departs from the conventions of the genre in some ways and uses few literary devices, which allows him to convey the decline of a world which is gradually being stripped of its old values and meanings. He uses the story of a postapocalyptic world to explore universal themes such as death, human nature and parent-child relationships, giving his bleak, violent narrative an important metaphysical dimension.

FURTHER REFLECTION

SOME QUESTIONS TO THINK ABOUT...

- Why do you think the child often refuses to speak?
- To what extent can the novel be considered dystopian?
- What role do the father's dreams and memories play in the story?
- To what extent does the description of the human condition given in the novel reflect absurdist philosophy? What comparisons can be drawn between *The Road* and the famous myth of Sisyphus?
- How does *The Road* portray God and religion?
- What vision of childhood does the author develop in his work?
- Temporal and spatial indicators are extremely vague in the novel. How does this reinforce its metaphysical dimension?
- In what ways does the novel's treatment of space and time contribute to the sense of

mounting violence?

- Analyse the novel's ending. To what extent can it be considered surprising? What are its implications?
- What are the similarities between *The Road* and Jack Kerouac's novel *On the Road*?

We want to hear from you!
Leave a comment on your online library
and share your favourite books on social media!

FURTHER READING

REFERENCE EDITION

- McCarthy, C. (2010) *The Road*. London: Picador.

ADAPTATION

- *The Road*. (2009) [Film]. John Hillcoat. Dir. USA: 2929 Productions.
  Much of *The Road* was filmed in New Orleans after Hurricane Katrina (2005). It is a very faithful adaptation, in terms of both the content and the tone of the novel. However, although its ending is very similar to the ending of the novel, it met with widespread criticism on the grounds that it is too "Hollywood". While the ostensibly happy ending seemed to work for the book, as readers came to it with a sense of relief, it was less well received in the film adaptation.

www.brightsummaries.com

Ebook EAN: 9782806279699

Paperback EAN: 9782806287588

Legal Deposit: D/2016/12603/648

This guide was written with the collaboration of
Marie-Sophie Wauquez and translated with the
collaboration of Rebecca Neal for the character study
of the cannibals, and for the sections "A postapocalyptic novel?", "Intertextuality" and "The metaphor
of religion".

Cover: © Primento

Digital conception by Primento, the digital partner of
publishers.

Printed in Great Britain
by Amazon

63698480R00037